LENTILES BIBLE NUMBERS *(LABV)*

The New Testament

The 23rd in the Series of

LENTILES ANNOTATED BIBLE VERSION

Published by:
Abiola Adaramola-Ariyehun

LENTILES BIBLE NUMBERS (LABV)

ISBNs: 979-8-88992-811-9 (paperback)
979-8-89342-844-5 (ebook)

Email: ellipticlens789@yahoo.com
www.chiralcentrebible.com
www.thebodyyofchrist.com

Lentiles Bible Numbers (LABV)

Shows the Biblical Meanings of Numbers

THE NEW TESTAMENT

The Book of Jude

CHAPTER 1

1 Jude the praise of the Lord; confession, the servant of Jesus Christ
anointed savior, and brother of James that supplants, undermines;
the heel, to them that are sanctified by God the Father, and
preserved in Jesus Christ anointed savior, and called:

$1_{6}, 5_{2}, 4_{5}, 9_{10}, 5_{2}, 2_{10}$:

Singleness $_{\text{man}}$, **Grace**$_{\text{witness\& support}}$, **Balance**$_{\text{grace}}$ **Fullness of Blessing** $_{\text{human government and law}}$, **Grace**$_{\text{witness\& support}}$, **Witness** $_{\text{human government and law}}$:

2 Mercy unto you, and peace, and love, be multiplied.

3_{10}, 2_{10}, 2_{10}, 2_{10}.

Perfection and Unity Human government & law, **Witness & Support** Commandment, **Witness & Support** Human government & law, **Witness & Support** Commandment.

[3]Beloved, when I gave all diligence to write unto you of the common salvation, it was needful for me to write unto you, and exhort you that ye should earnestly contend for the faith which was once delivered unto the saints.

1_{10}, 13_{10}, 9_{10}, 18_{10}.

Singleness$_{\text{Commandment}}$, **Rebellion &Divine Atonement** $_{\text{Human government \& law}}$, **Fullness of Blessing**$_{\text{Commandment}}$, **(Witness &Support x Fullness of Blessing)** $_{\text{Human government \& law}}$.

[4]For there are certain men crept in unawares, who were before of old ordained to this condemnation, ungodly men, turning the grace of our God into lasciviousness, and denying the only Lord God, and our Lord Jesus Christ anointed savior.

$8_{10}, 9_{10}, 2_{10}, 8_{10}, 6_{10}, 5_{2}.$

New beginning commandment, **Fullness of blessing** commandment, **Witness & Support** commandment, **New beginning** commandment, **Man** commandment, **Grace** witness & support.

5 I will therefore put you in remembrance, though ye once knew this, how that the Lord, having saved the people out of the land of Egypt that troubles or oppresses; anguish, afterward destroyed them that believed not.

$7_{10}, 5_{10}, 4_{10}, 10_{5}, 6_{10}.$

Divine Perfection $_{\text{commandment}}$, **Grace** $_{\text{commandment}}$, **Balance** $_{\text{commandment}}$, **Commandment** $_{\text{grace}}$, **Man**$_{\text{commandment}}$.

[6]And the angels which kept not their first estate, but left their own habitation, he hath reserved in everlasting chains under darkness unto the judgment of the great day.

9_{10}, 5_{10}, 15_{10}.

Fullness of Blessing$_{\text{commandment}}$, **Grace**$_{\text{commandment}}$, **(Commandment + Grace)**$_{\text{commandment}}$.

7Even as Sodom their secret; their cement; burning; the walled and
Gomorrha rebellious people; submersion, and the cities about
them in like manner, giving themselves over to fornication,
and going after strange flesh, are set forth for an example,
suffering the vengeance of eternal fire.

$3_7 2_3$, 8_{10}, 5_{10}, 5_{10}, 6_{10}, 6_{10}.

Completion completeness **Witness &Support** completion, **New Beginning** commandment, **Grace** commandment, **Grace** commandment, **Man** commandment, **Man** commandment.

[8]Likewise also these filthy dreamers defile the flesh, despise dominion, and speak evil of dignities.

8_{10}, 2_{10}, 5_{10}.

New Beginning commandments, **Witness & Support** commandment, **Grace** commandment.

9Yet Michael humble; poor the archangel, when contending
with the devil slanderer, false accuser the arch-enemy of man's spiritual
interest he disputed about the body of Moses taken out; drawn
forth; drawer out; one born, durst not bring against him a railing
accusation, but said, The Lord rebuke thee.

$2_2 2_{10}$, $5_{10} 7_8$, 8_{10}, 2_{10}, 4_{10}.

Witness & Support witness & support **Witness & Support** commandment , **Grace** commandment **Completeness** new beginning , **New Beginning** commandment , **Witness & Support** commandment , **Balance** commandment.

[10]But these speak evil of those things which they know not:
but what they know naturally, as brute beasts, in those
things they corrupt themselves.

11_{10}: 5_{10}, 3_{10}, 6_{10}.

Disperse$_{\text{Human government \& law}}$: **Grace** $_{\text{commandment}}$, **Completion** $_{\text{Human government \& law}}$, **Man** $_{\text{commandment}}$.

[11]Woe unto them! for they have gone in the way of Cain a possession; a spear; acquired, and ran greedily after the error of Balaam lord or ancient of the people; foreigner; glutton; the destruction of the peaople for reward, and perished in the gainsaying of Core baldness; ice; frost.

3_{10}! 9_5, 8_{13} 2_{10}, 7_3.

Completion commandment! **Fullness of Blessing** Grace, **New Beginning** Rebellion & Divine Atonement **Witness & Support** commandment, **Completeness** completion.

12These are spots in your feasts of charity, when they feast
with you, feeding themselves without fear: clouds they are
without water, carried about of winds; trees whose fruit
withereth, without fruit, twice witness and support; 2 x 1 dead,
plucked up by the roots;

$8_{10}, 5_{10}, 4_{10}: 5_{10}, 4_{10}; 4_{10}, 2_{10}, 1_5 1_{10}, 5_{10};$

New Beginning commandment, **Grace** commandment, **Balance** commandment: **Grace** commandment, **Balance** commandment; **Balance** commandment, **Witness & Support** commandment, **Singleness** grace **Singleness** commandment, **Grace** commandment ;

[13]Raging waves of the sea, foaming out their own shame; wandering stars, to whom is reserved the blackness of darkness for ever.

$5_{10}, 5_{10}; 2_{10}, 10_{10}.$

Grace Commandment, **Grace** Commandment; **Witness & Support** Commandment, **Human government & Law** Commandment.

[14]And Enoch dedicated; disciplined; initiated; teacher also, the seventh divine perfection or completeness; 7 x 1 from Adam earthy; red; mankind; firm, prophesied of these, saying, Behold, the Lord cometh with ten thousands 2 x 2 x 2 x 2 x 5 x 5 x 5 x 5 of his saints,

$2_4 1_{10}$, $2_6 2_4$, 3_{10}, 1_{10}, 1_{10}, $6_8\, 3_{10}$,

Witness & Support Balance Singleness Commandment , **Witness & Support Man Witness & Support Balance , Completion** Commandment , **Singleness** Commandment , **Singleness** Commandment , **Man New beginning Completion** Commandment ,

[15]To execute judgment upon all, and to convince all that are ungodly among them of all their ungodly deeds which they have ungodly committed, and of all their hard speeches which ungodly sinners have spoken against him.

5_{10}, 19_{10}, 13_{10}.

Grace $_{\text{Commandment}}$, (Commandment + Fullness of Blessing) $_{\text{Commandment}}$, (Commandment + Completion)$_{\text{Commandment}}$.

[16]These are murmurers, complainers, walking after their own lusts; and their mouth speaketh great swelling words, having men's persons in admiration because of advantage.

3_{10}, 1_{10}, 5_{10}; 7_{10}, 8_{10}.

Completion Commandment , **Singleness** Commandment , **Grace** Commandment ; **Completeness** Commandment , **New Beginning** Commandment .

17But, beloved, remember ye the words which were spoken
before of the apostles messengers; envoys of our Lord Jesus
Christ anointed savior;

1_{10}, 1_{10}, $11_2 5_2$;

Singleness Commandment , Singleness Commandment , Disperse witness & support Gracewitness & support ;

[18]How that they told you there should be mockers in the last time, who should walk after their own ungodly lusts.

13_{10}, 8_{10}.

Rebellion & Divine Atonement $_{\text{Commandment}}$, **New Beginning** $_{\text{Commandment}}$.

19These be they who separate themselves, sensual, having
not the Spirit.

6_{10}, 1_{10}, 4_{10}.

Man $_{\text{commandment}}$, **Singleness** $_{\text{commandment}}$, **Balance** $_{\text{commandment}}$.

[20]But ye, beloved, building up yourselves on your most holy
faith, praying in the Holy Ghost,

2_{10}, 1_{10}, 8_{10}, 5_{10},

Witness & Support $_{\text{commandment}}$, **Singleness** $_{\text{commandment}}$, **New Beginning** $_{\text{commandment}}$, **Grace** $_{\text{commandment}}$,

21 Keep yourselves in the love of God, looking for the mercy
of our Lord Jesus Christ anointed savior unto eternal life.

7_{10}, 9_{2} 3_{10}.

Completeness commandment , **Fullness of blessing** witness & support
Completion commandment .

[22]And of some have compassion, making a difference:

5_{10}, 3_{10}:

Grace $_{\text{commandment}}$, **Completion** $_{\text{commandment}}$:

[23]And others save with fear, pulling them out of the fire;
hating even the garment spotted by the flesh.

5_{10}, 6_{10}; 8_{10}.

Grace $_{\text{commandment}}$, **Man** $_{\text{commandment}}$; **New beginning** $_{\text{commandment}}$.

[24]Now unto him that is able to keep you from falling, and to present you faultless before the presence of his glory with exceeding joy,

11_{10}, 14_{10},

Disperse $_{\text{commandment}}$, (**Grace + Fullness of Blessing**) $_{\text{commandment}}$,

[25]To the only wise God our Saviour, be glory and majesty, dominion and power, both now and ever. Amen dependable; faithful; certain; true; firm.

$7_{10}, 4_{10}, 3_{10}, 4_{10} \cdot 1_{5}.$

Completeness commandment **, Balance** commandment **, Completion** commandment **, Balance** commandment**. Singleness** Grace**.**

End of the book Jude

LENTILES ANNOTATED BIBLE VERSION (LABV)

LENTILES ANNOTATED STUDY BIBLE-*KJV*

CHIRAL CENTRE LENTILES STUDY BIBLE*(LABV)*

WWW.CHIRALCENTREBIBLE.COM

LENTILES BIBLE THESAURUS-Literal & symbolic; left handed and right handed (www.thebodyyofchrist.com)

LENTILES BIBLE RODS*(LABV)*

LENTILES BIBLE MATRICES-*(KJV)*

LENTILES BIBLE CHORDS 1*(LABV)*

LENTILES BIBLE CHORDS 2*(LABV)*

LENTILES BIBLE CHROMOSOMES/NECKLACES*(LABV)*

ENANTIOMERS LENTILES STUDY BIBLE*(LABV)*

HEART RHYTHM LENTILES STUDY BIBLE*(LABV)*

LENTILES BIBLE LADDER*(LABV)*

LENTILES BIBLE SPRINGS*(LABV)*

THE BLOOD THAT SPEAKS LENTILES STUDY BIBLE*(LABV)*

THE PROCEEDING WORDS LENTILES STUDY BIBLE *(LABV)*

RHEMA LENTILES STUDY BIBLE *(LABV)*

LOGOS LENTILES STUDY BIBLE *(LABV)*

SYNTAX LENTILES STUDY BIBLE-*(LABV)*

SEMANTIC LENTILES STUDY BIBLE- *(LABV)*

SYLLABLES LENTILES STUDY BIBLE*(LABV)*

MUSTARD SEED LENTILES STUDY BIBLE*(LABV)*

RIDGES AND FURROWS LENTILES STUDY BIBLE*(LABV)*

OPTICAL ISOMERS LENTILES STUDY BIBLE*(LABV)*

STREAM ORDER /DENTRITES LENTILES STUDY BIBLE *(LABV)*

MERCY AND TRUTH MEETS TOGETHER LENTILES STUDY BIBLE*(LABV)*

RIGHTEOUSNESS KISSES PEACE LENTILES STUDY BIBLE*(LABV)*

LENTILES BIBLE NUMBERS*(LABV)*

CHRISTMAS TREE LENTILES STUDY BIBLE*(LABV)*

HONEYCOMB LENTILES STUDY BIBLE*(LABV)*

LENTILES BIBLE CHARTS

THE BUTTERFLY CHRISTIAN

COMMUNICATION IN THE INTELLECTUAL WORLD

COMMUNICATION IN THE SPIRIT WORLD

COMMUNICATION IN THE PHYSICAL WORLD

COMMUNICATION IN BIOLOGICAL WORLD

TYPES OF HEARTS

BEAUTIFUL ATTITUDES

CHARACTERISTICS OF LIVING THINGS

BROOKS OF THE BIBLE

SPIRITUAL BODY SYSTEM

THE FLESH VERSUS THE SPIRIT

COMINGS OF THE LORD JESUS CHRIST

COMPLETE KNOWLEDGE OF GOD

SPIRITUAL FOOD SOURCES

GATES OF ZION

THE CORNER STONE

MAGNETIZING FIELDS

LITERAL AND SYMBOLIC KNOWLEDGE

THE SPIRITUAL CELL

EFFECTS OF CARNALITY IN THE CHURCH

THE HEALED TREE

THE PROMISE LAND

INTELLIGENCE

THE JUSTICE OF GOD

SPIRITUAL PERIODIC TABLE

THE CHURCHES REPORT CARD

LENTILES BOOKS

THE THIRD DAY

THE ANATOMY AND PHYSIOLOGY OF BELIEVE AND FAITH

GOD OF RESTORATION

THE WISDOM OF GOD

THE ENCLOSED SPACE (*The human soul*)

About The Author

Abiola Deborah Adaramola-Ariyehun hails from Ekiti State, Nigeria in West Africa. She was born in Kano and had both Primary and Secondary Education in Kano State, Nigeria. She holds qualifications in Universities of Port-Harcourt, University of Calabar and University of Ibadan, Nigeria. Also Rutgers University NJ, University of Medicine & Dentistry New Jersey (UMDNJ) and Seton Hall Universities New Jersey USA inclusive. She founded Ellipses-Lentiles and published her first book titled: Abiola Deborah Lentiles Study Bible in 2016. She stands in awe of God's Wisdom, Personality and Power.

www.ingramcontent.com/pod-product-compliance
Lightning Source LLC
LaVergne TN
LVHW010512160826
845677LV00012B/2817